ARC TANGENT

Also by Eric Selland:

POETRY

The Condition of Music (Sink Press, 2000)
Inventions (Mindmade Books, 2007)
Still Lifes (Hank's Original Loose Gravel Press, 2012)

TRANSLATIONS

Yoshioka Minoru, *Kusudama* (Leech Books, 1991)
Takagai Hiroya, *Rush Mats* (Duration Press, 1999)
Takashi Hiraide, *The Guest Cat* (New Directions, 2014)

ARC TANGENT

Eric Selland

ISOBAR
PRESS

First published in 2014 by

Isobar Press
Sakura 2-21-23-202
Setagaya-ku
Tokyo 156-0053
Japan

http://isobarpress.com

ISBN 978-4-907359-01-0

© Eric Selland, 2014
All rights reserved.

ACKNOWLEDGEMENTS

Portions of 'Arc Tangent' first appeared in *Untitled: A Journal of Prose Poetry*, while some selections from 'Table of Primaries' first appeared in *26 Magazine*.

The cover features a diagram by EuYu (http://math.stackexchange.com/users/9246/euyu) which is part of his response on Math Stack Exchange to the topic 'Get Angle to Tangent that Intersects Point' (http://math.stackexchange.com/questions/205640/get-angle-to-tangent-that-intersects-point).

CONTENTS

Arc Tangent   7

Table of Primaries   37

Arc Tangent

*For first must dwelling pass away,
and order, and become deformed.*
Friedrich Hölderlin

*In the redeemed world, everything
would be as it is, and yet wholly other.*
Giorgio Agamben

How close I am to a question.

Every time I dance, a gift of a painted object arrives. In it is the world, condensed like one of the shorter sonata works for cello, and like it covered in darkness. The wet flesh of the inner folds beckons to me. Into it I plunge in hopes of losing all that which has been collected and become merely a burden to me. That which is remembered and not understood. More and more so the empty crates lining the orchards of the home. The dry place. Objects seek me out. The hand come to resemble itself in the moment, in the dance of the lost appendages. The immense, spectacled features of the composer. He died and lost his hand. As in a book with no letters read out of the memory. Like the objects that speak in his dreams, he is swift to leave. Of their own accord they reach out and grasp him. The usual process of making a painting. This is the moment in which the shadow of the dream resembled the shadow of the poem.

The grasping hand comes to be itself. Grasped. In the process of making. It comes to resemble itself. The shadow of a hand. Hegel speaks of the movement of the absolute as the movement of a name that is only a meaningless sound. Whoever experiences disgust has in some way recognized himself. But only insofar as it was in the voice, that is, insofar as it always already belongs to the past. The faults are inseparable from the substance. Repair or alteration is often a process involving pain. The sense that the truth of a thing has been somehow violated in having spoken of it. The subject which is not really a subject. The rift between self and world passes in turn through the self.

It bears witness to neither one nor the other. What cannot be stated, what cannot be archived, is the language in which the author succeeds in bearing witness to his incapacity to speak. But what does it mean to speak in a remaining language? Often it seems as though one were like another. They have always been there. I do not look at them. The passage between the outside and the inside. Now the twentieth century will be emptied. I do not exclude machines. Machines mean complexity. And then there are the advanced processes. Thus the higher terms in the equation diminish more rapidly than if there were no obstacle, but the beginning terms are unaffected. Accordingly, the terms in the summation diminish on both ends. Everything is already broken off

Outside the sentence
Rain is falling
As if a porous film
Set between waking and sleep.

The parched mouth and
Uneasiness of night remain.
It dissolves. The sickness does not dissolve.

Always the expected visit
The order to awaken
And selection

The water mark
Mirror in my sleep
Measuring the presence of light.

So in shame we are consigned to something from which we cannot in any way distance ourselves.

The slipper Artaud held in his mouth at the moment just before his death.

What remains is physical sensation
Physical memory
Connection to natural landscape

The priority of the whole

It is as if we are being told that it is only through the distortion of normative reality that we are capable of reaching its underlying truth.

Nevertheless, he confessed his only recurring dream – a darkened room and a window's broken shutter through which an intruder attempts to enter. The enclosure. This time there was a complexity to the interior – many hallways and turns . . .

As levels are added and topography evolves, resembling the profile of a cityscape, the difference between the most positive and most negative features increases beyond the depth of focus.

The light is softer now, oozes honey-colored onto the myrtle and emerald ivy. Before the face, I find myself exposed. This indispensable circumstance. The meal again becomes complex. The words abruptly following one another.

But there are other factors, other voices

To explain nothing at all

Since the product must vanish, either or both of the factors must be equal to zero. Setting the first factor to zero gives the equation of a circle. The second factor gives the equation of an ellipse.

No longer is there a fabric
But merely division
At the very place once occupied
There is now fragmentation

The fact that in it
Nothing is immediate
The divide
Everything is refracted, significant,
Withdrawn.
The rendering indifferent of the material
The moment of distress in the later period

Where longing itself is changed as it plunges from the dream into appearance. Let us consider the observers moving with constant relative speed. Or consider a plane electromagnetic wave whose space-time dependence is of a particular form. The apparatus mounted on a rigid support that can be rotated about a vertical axis. That one lives in confrontation and is yet removed. The conversation. We speak to him only when all speech has ceased.

What are the words
That are spoken
Lighting the candles
Covering the eyes
The sun sinks
Voices rising
Out of the silence.

These are the generations
Every plant reaching
Its form
To each thing its name.

The work of sleep
How can we see what we no longer see

That night I dreamed about the entrance, barely large enough to squeeze the precious cargo through. The group labored into the night, removing the metallic cushions from the movable parts on the interior of the machine.

Night squeaks past
The machinery
Breath shortens under mask

The mechanical parts
Are discarded –
Outside, blackbirds scatter after rain

Entering history
Bits and pieces of decayed matter
Become unconcealed

The structure of the piece is Mozartean, though its source unknown. Sound of vacuum cleaner drowns out all for a moment. One wonders if there is a difference. Heat buildup in comparison to exterior outstanding. Terms and positions. I can only name objects. I can only speak of them. I cannot assert them. Of course, there is always a sense in which, in seeing, one actually does not see at all. In later years I tried referring to it as a topological labyrinth, but actually the neighborhood was a slum. There must be objects. That is how a picture is attached to reality; it reaches right out to it. The ants come into the house in search of moisture.

Before confronting the question
Disturbance
                        A disturbance between two fields
The impossibility of reaching the place where one already is

The door never opens
The double figure of the Messiah

Privation is like a face
Everything is complicated
In being there

The way into questioning

In the library of images
The steps

           A sense of stillness
           Desire for stillness

                  Clay figures
                  Surrounding the room

The flowers and shrubs
Are silent

The lyric exfoliation of identity

Is the hurt named
      Numbing
           Numbering the years

Stopped in at the fish market for a bite to eat and there was M sitting in a far corner of the room, her appearance essentially unchanged from the last time I saw her twenty years ago. What does the eye see? The majority of functional memory hidden somewhere below the surface.

How many times is bad judgment required. An accumulation of light imprints the desired shape on the surface, the final product obtained through a process of searing and cutting, followed by growth of an upper layer.

Man is just this container
Of shadow in offspring
Ready to hand

A universe
The size of a pin
I found one inside you

Like a tremendous faucet
Turning on and off
The color of raspberry

Only there can eternity be found
Muscular spasm
Clouded collapse

Kafka's parable of the travelers boarding a stalled train, the view from the windows occluded.

I was found by those who did not seek me

Moonlight on artificial lake. Who are these beings within us? The terminus in itself encloses the nucleus. A crisis in terms. What is understood is not an intention. It is as if the letters wrote themselves on the tablets. But what does it mean to nourish? The self pared down to a gnarled stump, a mere accumulation of its painful truths. A closing of figures.

At the opposite end of the palace stood the cabinet of wonder, containing rocks of an unusual shape, coins, stuffed animals, mechanical dolls, paintings and miniatures, and an enormous egg. How to make the fragments speak. There is for man an original container. Even death is laid bare.

Marks outside the prohibited zone
We see darkness
Once again the difference
As movement, it gives itself
The chair must encounter something

That we were always perceiving in folds, grasping figures without objects. He had arrived beyond the point of understanding. So goes the theory . . . but I still find that I am working in the dark. But then we find another question intruding upon us. Seamless exposure. The complex meaning of collapse. Patterns have existed or disappeared. The notion of a line contained on a field of infinitely small sections, where exposure burns and obliterates. Rather is everything picture and movement, species and instance. Whatever belongs to the tree is included. All this in its entirety. What I encounter is the tree itself. The landscape of the wound.

This is when I learned how to make the sound of a mourning dove by cupping the hands, and guiding the air through the space between the thumbs, using a motion with the forefingers of the left hand to produce the precise tones of the bird's call. Those were the colder days in summer, rust and magenta, damp rot of the roots. A night bird chatters.

Wild mustard blooms off highway
After darkness
Other points on spectrum

Her interests lie in the process of decay and deterioration. Elsewhere the book as source. Reference to tearing, cutting, slicing and stripping. To re-enter the life through the book. Gradually the people reappear. Tomoko in her tight leopard-skin outfit waiting in the lobby of the stock exchange. And then the dream again of the empty room, semi-darkness, but this time two sides of the building open to the outside, providing a vantage point over the streams of walkers passing through the street. The moment one sees a kind of object and is at peace with that.

Each day at 3:00 the foreign workers would take their coffee at the hotel on the wide boulevard across from the palace moat, and at exactly 3:15 a horse-drawn coach would canter down the way, footmen in eighteenth-century attire attached to the back as if two mechanical dolls, and enter through a side gate of the forbidden complex. The occasion was at once surprising and banal.

Sun drips into the site
Of tree's dislocation
After rain, a fullness
And of the heart yet something calls
From the possible
The cold yet active
World without memory

Birds are absent
I think of the cold
Of desire
Of childhood memory
The coast pouring out its nourishment
And I think of where to go

They were vessels each moment
Disorderly
The synchronous white
I see you no longer
For that is time
And image – no image
In your mind
And I have my own

As if my whole life
Were a single note
Heard from the dark root

Of which there remains no trace
The process of translation
Which makes possible the reading
Of this text at all
The source obliterated in the process

Living in a landscape of signs
A landscape of meanings
And the loss of those meanings

Shadow of housefly huge
Against paper screen

        The actual insect
        Withholding its figure

In the breech
Behind nylon

        Wood, stone and other
        Natural materials mix

The outside framed
Yet hidden in this season

And now the blackness extends
A geology of the name
Its abysmal interior
Room, April, umbrella, night

The sublation of the individual moment in the totality
Nothing, finally, is resolved

But the changes of character within a single movement –
even within its smaller sections

Where the right hand crosses over

All the images are broken
The people, also broken
Return to their houses
The blackened houses

Alteration of image. To simplify the body in the event it bears. The exterior is rather simple and unarticulated, while the sides facing the plaza display a wide variety of forms and finishes. The long gaze is fastened on the condemned. Still you are inside me, held in sleep, in unlikely remembrance. Certain passages where the music seems to be suspended. Number in landscape. The problems seemed to become even more complex over time, and ultimately unresolvable.

There are multiple levels, some not detectable. One may acquiesce to the tendency of the smallest notes. The thought expressed which is of a meandering. It carries the reticles through a series of operations that use carriers moving along three axes. M enters in flimsy dress, the optical reflectance of her face, the four layers held in suspension. Conductive and transparent. The phase shift of the light. The form held only in its final botanical image – water; sleep. Specific light of the dream. Hollow sound of bamboo flute; shadows framed in lattice and glow of yard.

It is only now that we come to language, like a huge river of elements. Refracted light. Deformation of figures and human faces. Avenue of approximate plane. The gradual process of unfolding. Steps heard, but he is not here.

It's part of the puzzle, as vanishing they go away. The space between people. Then the page turns. The conclusion that light is an electromagnetic disturbance. As in tonal distribution – nevertheless the vertical shot as it passes through the causal rupture of time or dimension. Brief instant in which the shadow of the one resembles the other.

A conversation about K. The weight on the left side almost unbearable. The possibility that recapitulation might begin on a different degree. And since variation does not change all features but preserves some of them, distantly related motive forms might sound incoherent. The revoked time no longer has a goal, leads nowhere, the cadence losing itself entirely. I call to mind what I have done. Hence I must draw myself into doubt.

The source from which the fragment speaks.

Because we have talked too much
As if heard
That we know it is enigma

The idea that the whole flow of time
Could be interrupted

Where writing begins

Yet there is unity in a kind of dividing up. Now history becomes possible, as light comes back across the layer, only scattered groups of notes remaining. The articulation of distance. Something profoundly hidden in that spoken between people. The canonic passage beginning the E-flat section. One brings the other with it, one lets the other go.

The return, so to speak, is dissolved. Such reduction of human features. But the configuration is a gift. Only figure. Other demands – a work and labor by which one transforms oneself. We note here the figures of costume and veil. The vanishing faces. The intersection of different worlds. But is the inner process, the experience of color, imaginable? A practice of the whole bearing of its own knowledge. So we shall proceed; thus the bridge, uniting the two parts.

They are feelings, and thus misunderstood.

The strength goes out of the hand
In this I am alone

    Association   perhaps

                    Correspondence

                            The meeting

        Something undergone

           With   the other

But never the communal

        Not the communal as source

                  Certainly not

Particles gather
    And then disperse

        It is the shadow that is the center

More and more not
The same
    Not
 Like that

                Is it the poem?

Plain things
And beings as things
Measure and comparison have fled

Only there (in the past) can life be arranged

What it means to be alone
But the world itself
    Embraces me

    A misreading
        On my part
            Perhaps

                It was not
                Clarity
                Not even
                Possibly
                Music

                But everything

                Measuring the difference
                Between light and dark

                    Coherent light

The old sign with the city's name
Written vertically
Protrudes from the crumbling movie theater

Last train out:
Construction sounds

Two jets perpetually float
In view of the verandah

Later silence
Except for occasional rumble
On tracks

But the moment will come when a man looks up and in a flash sees both pictures at once.

Not influence, but dialogue

Impromptu: how the word attracts

Henceforth there is no recurrence

The next question no longer concerns the threshold

Ready, not seeking, he goes his way

Nevertheless, he ventures to do this

Table of Primaries

*How far removed is their hidden meaning
from revelation, how close can it be brought
by the knowledge of its remoteness.*
Walter Benjamin

*Sometimes you run out of notes
and you just have to play a sound.*
Miles Davis

The large granite rock is impaled atop the metallic structure, giving the illusion of balance. Through the metal frame can be seen a body of water, sleek buildings of glass and occasional flying birds of various species. The rock hangs in the air, displaced from its original position. The metal spars defy description, or definition. One would like the rock to come down. One would like the rock to be beautiful, to be simply a rock, to return somewhere – perhaps to some sense of belonging. Or this very opacity; the very weight and impossibility of interpretation that is the object's point.

The nude figure
In the deserted courtyard
The curve of the back

For what is this self that concerns the poet so much?
It is also a stranger.
Early on, I learned the art of disguise.

But we are contemporaries
We are at the end point
The space of history

He had become detached from the hand.
The tension between excess and restraint,
Exhibitionism and concealment.

What is it, really, to be authentic?

All I have ever done is move back and forth. Narrow streets of the old city cluttered with used bookstores and cafés, sleep pressing on the body, and thirst, cumbersome volumes of Chinese classics stacked on end. She orders sweet bean paste and green tea, and opens her book. The book she had not planned on buying. The book that came to her. Experience means to obtain something along the way.

Orientation of the lattice
Concept of diffusion
The distance takes place
This too demands an explanation
The pattern repeated

Somewhere in here there's a way to reverse the polarity of this thing, but it's hidden. Pull up on this one and the oxygen sensor goes to zero. And it's not supposed to do that. It doesn't do any good. So you can see the damned thing. You want a sound, a kind of sound. I have hardly begun.

Much in the spoken statements has a purely musical value. The process repeated till the end of the line then snap; drum snare, the accentuated note. As if I were a part of the rock. And I remember Queequeg and the little rooming house. All the intricate markings on the body. Swirls in the driftwood. Twisting, turning back. Thinkin', not talkin'. At first he depended on the use of mathematical models of disorder. The two beams hitting the mark. Phase difference. To have experienced the street was like reading a text. You could go where you wanted and hear all this great shit. The form of distinction.

A series of oddly shaped boxes, each labeled with its corresponding part – core, pedestal, plate and so on. The boundary between station and destination. There was a nostalgia not only for the person, but for what his life signified. Up close in the figure. Each object in a sense personified by its grammatical status within the sentence. The series of monuments dotting the coast produce a mandala-like structure on the map. But the mouth keeps moving despite death. The steps described definitively in the book. I thought the secret must be hidden in just this one word. That gift is called distance. There should be a pleasure in the hearing of it. Always too much or too little in the said. But how to speak of these things.

Only now can the basic word be put together
The center of the visible spectrum
The thing in itself

The force of these objects. That there is a strange kind of beauty in the steel frame construction bringing form to a building, the hills beyond visible through the skeletal shape. The sad beauty of the afternoon, and the automobiles, providing motion, endless motion. That we call it time and no matter how we try cannot understand.

Up till 2:00 a.m. listening
To the caller's voice
First angry, now desperate

Then out for a breath
Of fresh air to see
Three deer in the city street
Come down from the hills
In this almost sacred quiet

The distances are more varied
First order of light
Trying to clarify what the questions are

In the dark she cut imperfectly. We see animals and insects, bubbles on the surface. There is a horizon line, but it doesn't relate to the forms. Unmistakable passages of color, change, distinction (dissection), and one or two individual prints. In other words, what happens. That is to speak, not be concerned. Sounds, durations, attacks and delays. Because the words themselves are notation. An impulse toward non-obstruction.

At what point can we withdraw
I remember taking a long walk
There are seagulls
Not talking is something we do
Though indispensable to each other
Both are impenetrable

There is no real place, whereas
The contemporary
Would be quite different
Discreet is not being appreciative
Art has its own tradition
And where work is made

That is why
The ordinating phenomena
As tones vibrate
Explain the complete absence of weight
What you see not coming from there
Is applied, and gives no clue

How often they perform
At a warehouse
Like sleeping giants
Hardly breathing
As the others were leaving
I turned for a last look

The simple life lay somewhere beyond reach. This life from which I cannot escape. The city is filled with memory, and yet it is not really a choice, only a recognition. And then the words would not come. I once thought that I had plenty of time, but soon enough that misconception would be corrected. A musician knows something about time – keeping time, counting the beat. Something that slips away. For the first time he heard the clarinetist's breath inserted between measures. The person arrives in the midst of life's conditions. History as a dislocation or interruption of the normal state of affairs. That I was trying and it was very difficult not to bring in today's perspective. In either case I am not sure of understanding.

That we speak of sentences now in itself seems strange, and yet we go on talking. For a long time I dreamed of the rock; how it housed the elements, and over time, almost imperceptibly dissolved. Grains of rice overflowed from the torn sacks spilled out into the hallway. The rooms extended beyond the point where the outer wall originally ought to have been, hence, hanging in thin air. These rooms were neat to perfection, one housing rows of meticulously regimented files, the other containing an imposing oak table where the counselors were to hold their meetings. Where inner life itself becomes the site of Hegelian opposites.

This is the family of men with beards who wear hats. Carefully they search the horizon, checking the rows of identical houses for an open window, a familiar sound. Now the park is empty and the men are alone. They do not sit on the benches, but walk slowly along the lonely walkways like overgrown pigeons, their black coattails flapping in the breeze. The sky darkens. Someone calls out an almost familiar name. The men look up in unison.

A theme I have always played. He lived within the protective confines of an assumed normality. Like a man carrying a secret identity, he passed through the streets performing his daily routine. A series of false starts. A truth that resists in revealing. The life of the house. The sensation such that this would be completely human. The two types appearing in the dream. In the nameless city. The figure in the dream unattainable. The human reality of the present in all its brokenness. And that moment in time framed by his sudden departure. And the cold light of residence. The dark recesses of the house.

It begins with habitation.
Things are apprehended as solid substances.
The requirement that everyone speak was dropped.
The movements of birds and their hidden meanings.

Some lost work has been reconstituted more or less
                                                unchanged.
A cartographic mural made of paint and industrial tape.
I am finding I belong to neither world.
The movement comes from without.

Precedes even its objective forms. The approach of the other is an initiative I undergo. His oscillations between abstraction and representation, the geometric and the organic. The objects composed of or resembling items of daily use. Two oblong impressions in the rock. The hand suspended. His transient sensations of seeing across an extended space. In a process of incessant rebuilding. Its two contrapuntal movements – the descending body and the ascending stairs. He had set himself a task of more perplexing order. I am delighted to see that you have a proper nose. For reasons that will become clear later, the king is the most important piece. The cage immediately locates its space in the artificial. The figure on the empty stage.

How the figure disturbs. The self-imposed impossible. By which the subject opens itself to objects and to things. The thesis that there is an openness beneath or prior to that openness. There is an exposure to exteriority itself. Then from the start I am another. The notion of the immediate. The sense of the unfinished. But there is no way to construct a key. The unsayable. I was thinking about the immensity of the present, and of one's own present situation; the day-to-day reality and how it too is incomprehensible. The perplexity of going on. Departure and arrival; light and shadow. Scraps of memory beginning to drift through the outlying regions of the mind. Sometimes it seemed as if the veil would part. Not the question regarding the complex form of the capital. Again, the circular argument. An unbroken succession of strange faces emerging. The realization that he did not belong in this city, nor, indeed, anywhere else in the world.

The dark corridor of childhood. And in adulthood also, confusion of growth. I remember the quiet and the cold of that autumn evening, the silhouette of my parents' house in the distance, and the sound of blackbirds. The shadows of the large trees swelling beyond the height of the fence and my own anxiety. That one might be companioned by this absent companion. No finality; no release. He liked watching the trains, their reassuring arrival and departure. The comfort of turning the page.

For instance I am walking alone through the city and pass through old Chinatown. Rattle of the mahjong pieces emerging from the alley. Gradually meaning returns. The incarnation of the logos. At the end point, a music of not knowing. A system gradually folds in upon itself. Audrey Hepburn's eyes, the form of the fire escape – there are certain registers that can no longer be heard.

I speak of a certain dilemma
Between value and contingency
A form of refusal

Story of the hand
The broken story
Of the worn face of the rock
It did not provide an entrance

Enter into unknowing

I come to know the margins
Where the things revealed
Are stripped naked

The dance in the nude
A ritual too
The hand as a mnemonic device

I conceive of a number of objects
Their outlines drawn as if a horizon
Between shadow and light.
It is natural to pass from one to the other.

What does it mean to draw an object
What does a person see
How does one hold it
In the mind as well as the hand.

I am thinking of a subject
What was the question
I can only provide you with a range of methods,
An approach. The textual universe.

But there are choices.
To speak into history.
There were, first of all, the facts of a life
The textures of a life
A line drawn into itself.

The failure of either system to provide a home

And home, so it is,
Absorbed in the ordinary
Like the seaside town nearby
The waves breaking rhythmically on shore –
And the shops,
A place to walk
As if we had somewhere to go.

I remember the walks along the beach
At Aptos as a child
The broken ship in the distance
The great rumble of the sea a comfort.

I have a question that is unanswered.

What do I say?
I don't know what to say.
I am not satisfied with any answers.
Reading backwards results in revelation.

The fact of the singular.
His love of accident and spontaneity
In which the wood is seen as something alive –
To hold to a structure but not be bound

Like an object abides in the plasticity of an aspect. A setting that determines coordinates. The attack and decay of each instrument. As the size of the image decreases, the scale of the lens becomes huge. A natural crystalline structure occurs. By rotating individual elements, the effects are averaged out. The image, passed through a thin silicon membrane, is carefully stitched together. Chamber air pressure, flow and turbulence. Table deformation related to backlash. It was discovered that stage pads may scratch the ceramic coated base plate. Optical degradation. A prediction produced under the wrong assumptions. Critical dimension. Multicolored dots distributed across the map. The iterative matrix. The isolated feature produces a frown. I have now developed a method which I believe may extricate us from this impasse, a method that will require roughly the remainder of our lives. It is not a question of an effect undergoing its cause. A transgression that opens up a whole new way of being. Certainly what happens happens in place. This movement, this apparent disorder. Our understanding is not enough to comprehend the definition. Then the other – the original rupture.

We recognize, or assume, that different errors have different spatial signatures. The painful thrust into history, the scar across the cityscape. He would eventually adopt the formal vocabulary of these small objects, portraits in miniature, windows on nothing. The texts are approached in an increasingly visual, and even spatial manner. The relationship to the materials and the tools, how ink interacts with the page, the quality of the notebook and paper, the spatial positioning of the textual fragments, and finally the studio or workspace, table and lighting most appropriate in performing the final fitting process. A call to being that is so immediate and so necessary as to require an absolute distance. We had to piece together the fragments of a world constantly changing. The figure standing in the empty square. Even the difficulties come very quickly, and in some sense almost immediately. That in change I am seeing today her almost childlike face. It is the dream itself.

From the very beginning the schism was present. This is why there is no rest. He lived on various turns of phrase. Hence the search for magnitude, the sense of ease in complexity and a decisive execution of punctuation. Apparently, he was unaccustomed to writing. I am thinking about a letter, his confession about calculation. In face of their naked presence one speaks, and it seems with good reason. The questions all have become technical ones. He makes self-doubt into the highest form of art. There were the things, for instance, he wished to appropriate into his own understanding. The things that could not be kept away except in sleep. One makes it a concept. The absurd. There must be no stray light.

In the dream I am reunited with K, who expresses her profound sadness and disappointment in life. I offer her my sympathy and suggest we speak further. I am at a bank depositing a large amount of cash, which, surprisingly, has been lost by a homeless person. (I rationalize my having adopted the funds by the fact that this person cannot now be located.) Upon reaching the teller window, I speak to the Japanese teller in his own language, at which point he bursts out laughing uncontrollably. All this has been happening as I await K, but when I turn around she is gone. All this time I had felt a certain tinge of guilt at having ignored her letters all these years. But after all, it was she who had left. And the party of people I had left to go to the bank – who were they? I have no memory of their faces. What does it mean to have met K after all these years? Her face appeared somewhat aged, and tired. Indeed, she had grown tired of the world.

The poverty of being in between these two selves, these two times. And yet which in itself was a kind of absence. My life is a whole series of contradictions. Again I dream of C. To think there was a time when all the oppositions came together in one comprehensive whole – a great matrix of ideals and activity. Things fall apart. The image in various stages of disappearance. More and more I am absorbed in K's world. Of this there are signs. The once calm surface becomes disturbed. It is not enough to speak of proximity. Assuming one would want to keep up any correspondence at all. But this, too, has its difficulties.

Everyone carries a room inside him. Yesterday I ran into C for the first time in many months. He had returned in September from a research trip overseas but was now despondent, insisting to me that he should have stayed. It was at this moment that I realized my experience of returning to this country after years living abroad had been much the same. And now I see that a part of me never truly returned. In effect, I have lived out much of my life as if I were not actually here. In a way, I was never wholly present. But on the other hand, perhaps one is never wholly present in the world. The very notion of turning back.

We read this story in pieces
Like a kind of life
Seen from a great distance

His resistance to the natural
The garden chairs at the summer house
Sometimes not thinking
Dialect of the hand
Where S is the vector of incident light.

That decisions were made
That a way was taken
Kafka's axiom
That there is an infinite amount of hope,
But not for us.

I can no longer speak.
Her naked body sprawled out
Under the footlights.
The body of the text
Its place in the ritual.

There is always something peculiar that informs, ruptures or disrupts. Unfolds within the figure of the face. But the self cannot be reproduced. The tonal center rarely changes if there is one at all – in the moment of departure it is rendered strange and familiar. He writes as someone exposed. We imagine him an extra. The violence and power with which the voice penetrated me. The corpus of the disrupted self. In the dream the river is overflowing. It fills the green valley which the settlers had come to call home. I look into the transparent water and prepare to jump in.

I am speaking of a kind of fluidity,
Non-linearity of time

In another dream I am part of a commando raid on what appears to be a large research facility. With me is my wife, carrying the same automatic assault rifle that we all do. All goes well until my wife and I are suddenly ambushed in a hallway by two soldiers from the other side. They are two dear old friends (one of them dead long ago). We hesitate a moment, but then knowing that we will be taken prisoner otherwise, we shoot them dead with several bursts from our automatic weapons. The item it had been so important for us to retrieve and protect is now revealed – a bucket of clear water.

Where are we now
At the story of our thinking
The *coincidentia oppositorum*

Binding / concealing
Each thing itself returned to itself
What is and what is not a sentence

Immediately we find ourselves grappling with the question
Is this a sentence?
The filter checks the attributes.

There is a word I do not understand
It is a common word
A kind of sign.

I cannot say it
The essential word.

When the mask is peeled off
Will I be recognizable to myself?

Somewhere in the margins
To create a work.

A Note on Sources

Major sources: Theodor Adorno, *Philosophy of Modern Music* and *Beethoven: The Philosophy of Music*; Giorgio Agamben, various works; Louis Breger, *Freud: Darkness in the Midst of Vision*; Martin Buber, *I and Thou*; Holland Cotter, 'Trade Center Studios were Lost, but the Artists Get their Day,' *The New York Times*, December 3, 2001; Martin Heidegger, *What Is Called Thinking* and *Poetry, Language, and Thought*; Emmanuel Levinas, *Otherwise than Being* and other texts; Kazuo Ono, notes on Butoh; Tōru Takemitsu, *Confronting Silence*; Shūzō Takiguchi (as translated by Myriam Sas in *Fault Lines: Cultural Memory and Japanese Surrealism*); Minoru Yoshioka, *Umayahashi Nikki*. I have also used material and terminology from the fields of optics and semiconductor production encountered in my work as a technical translator.

www.ingramcontent.com/pod-product-compliance
Lightning Source LLC
Chambersburg PA
CBHW031214090426
42736CB00009B/916